MY FIRST BOOK OF Irish Animals

Best wishes,
Juanita Browne

Juanita Browne

Illustrated by Aoife Quinn

Acknowledgements

Sincere thanks to all those generous people who supported the publication of this book including the following: Isabell Smyth, Amanda Ryan, Michael Starrett, the Heritage Council; Bridget Loughlin and Kildare County Council; Ciara Baker; Moira Behan; Sean, Alison, Amy, Fiona and George Browne; Judith Browne, Brian Callan, Denis Clohessy, Seamus Connolly, Bríga Connolly, Juan Donnelly Hermera, Una and Ben Donnelly; Terry Donnelly, Colum Doyle, Sky and Eva Dunne; Rebecca Gale, Mary Gallagher, Bill Smyth RIP, Deirdre Halloran, Colin Lawton, John Lusby, Vera and Pat Lysaght, John Murray, Isobel O'Callaghan, Patrick J O'Keeffe, Caoimhín O'Murchú, Vern Power, Cailum Sheehy, Ray Swan, Seamus Sweeney, Fr. Leonard Taylor, Maureen and Dominic Timpson, Sophie Van Lonkhuyzen, and Teresa Walsh.

Thanks to Aoife Quinn for supplying her wonderful watercolour illustrations; Ray O'Sullivan for his lovely design; Aoife Carey for editing the promotional video for this book; and to Cepa Giblin for her long-running support. To the brilliant Conor Kelleher for sharing his knowledge for so many years; and Julian Reynolds for giving his time and encouragement.

Finally, of course, huge hugs and thanks to my husband Joe, my sons Ben and John, and all my family, for their support and love.

📷 PHOTOGRAPH CREDITS

p.8 Red Squirrel leaping, Crossing the Line Productions; p.19 Badger sett by Maria Archbold Cole; p. 22 Pine Marten climbing, Noel Marry; p.17 Leveret and p.22 Pine Marten kit courtesy of Dan Donoher, Kildare Animal Foundation Wildlife Unit.

p. 6 Brown Rat, Heiko Kiera/Shutterstock; p. 8 Grey Squirrel, Giedriius/Shutterstock; p.29 Red Deer, Matt Gibson/Shutterstock; p. 33 Fallow Deer, Matt Gibson/Shutterstock; p. 40 Grey Seal, Nicram Sabod/Shutterstock; p. 49 Bottlenose dolphins, Tory Kallman/Shutterstock; p. 53 Humpback Whale, Paul S. Wolf/Shutterstock.

Other images by Juanita Browne.

For Ben and John
x

Published in 2014 by
Juanita Browne,
Browne Books, Calverstown,
Kilcullen, Co. Kildare, Ireland.
email: jbrownebooks@gmail.com

ISBN: 978-0-9550594-1-4

Text © Juanita Browne
Illustrations © Aoife Quinn
Designer: Ray O'Sullivan – Pixelpress.ie
Printed by Turners, Longford, Ireland.

A catalogue record for this book is available from the British Library

All rights reserved. No part of this publication may be reproduced or transmitted in any form or by any means, electronic or manual, including photocopy, recording or any information storage or retrieval system without permission in writing from Juanita Browne.

Supported by

Contents

Wood Mouse	6	
Red Squirrel	8	
Hedgehog	10	
Pygmy Shrew	12	
Rabbit	14	
Irish Mountain Hare	16	
Badger	18	
Otter	20	
Pine Marten	22	
Irish Stoat	24	
Fox	26	
Red Deer	28	

Sika Deer	30
Fallow Deer	32
Common Pipistrelle Bat	34
Brown Long-eared Bat	36
Lesser Horseshoe Bat	38
Grey Seal	40
Harbour Seal	42
Harbour Porpoise	44
Common Dolphin	46
Bottlenose Dolphin	48
Killer Whale	50
Humpback Whale	52
Fin Whale	54
Blue Whale	56

Wood Mouse

An Luch Fhéir

Wood Mice live in long burrows underground. They are actually very clean animals. They have separate areas in their burrow system in which to store food, sleep or to use as a toilet.

They are 'nocturnal' which means they sleep during the day and are active at night. When it gets dark, they come out of their burrows to find food. They eat seeds, grains, berries, mushrooms, acorns, insects, snails, and worms. They have strong sharp teeth that can cut through the shells of nuts and other hard foods.

Look at those ears!

The Wood Mouse has very good hearing. They communicate with each other using high-pitched squeaks humans can't hear.

Brown Rat

Like other rodents such as the Brown Rat and the Bank Vole, the Wood Mouse is an important food for many other animals. Barn Owl, Kestrel, Pine Marten, Stoat, and Fox all eat mice and rats. If we had no rodents, we wouldn't have these beautiful animals either! And, of course, if we didn't have predators, we would be overrun by rodents!

SIZE

The Wood Mouse has big eyes and very good eyesight to help it find its way after dark, when it is safer for it to be out of its burrow.

Its long sensitive whiskers help it to feel its surroundings even in complete darkness.

Mice have great balance and can walk along narrow wires or scale rough walls and trees. They can also jump from heights of over 3 metres and land on the ground without hurting themselves!

Red Squirrel

Iora rua

There are two types of squirrel in Ireland, the Red Squirrel and the Grey Squirrel. They can be found in our gardens and city parks as well as hedgerows and forests.

Squirrels eat nuts, berries, pine cones, beech mast, pollen, buds, shoots and mushrooms.

Grey squirrels are bigger and heavier than the Reds and don't have long ear tufts. Greys spend more time on the ground than Red Squirrels.

Red Squirrels are great acrobats! They can leap from branch to branch and run quickly up and down the trunks of trees.

Squirrels make a spherical nest in a tree called a 'drey', using twigs, grass and leaves. This is where they sleep and have their babies.

DID YOU KNOW? Zzzzzz....

Squirrels don't hibernate during winter. In autumn they collect lots of acorns and other foods and store them in lots of different hiding places for the winter ahead when food is scarce. This means they don't have to spend lots of time out and about searching for food in cold weather. Instead they can spend much of their time in their cosy dreys sleeping. When they're hungry, they can just run out quickly to collect food from a secret stash.

During winter, the Red Squirrel grows long fluffy ear tufts and its fur coat gets much thicker to protect it from the cold.

SIZE

Hedgehog

Gráinneog

The Hedgehog makes its home in woodlands, hedgerows and gardens. It is usually active after dark. Each night it can cover large distances of up to three kilometres, while it searches for food – insects, slugs, worms, caterpillars and fruit.

It is a good idea to leave holes at the bottom of your garden fence to allow your local hedgehogs to move between gardens.

In summer the mother gives birth to around four babies. When they are about a month old, their mother leads them out of their nest and they learn to find food by copying Mum.

Although difficult to see under its coat of spines, the Hedgehog does have legs! They can run quite quickly when they have to, and they can swim, too.

A suit of Armour!

The Hedgehog has over 5,000 spines on its back. If it needs to protect itself, it can roll itself into a tight ball of spines – completely hiding its head and soft belly.

In winter, when there is less food about, the Hedgehog has a clever way to survive – it hibernates. This means it goes into a deep sleep so that it uses less energy and can live off its body fat until warmer spring weather arrives.

During hibernation the Hedgehog's body temperature drops to about 4°c and its heart beat slows from over 200 beats per minute to just 5bpm.

Pygmy Shrew

Dallóg fhraoigh

The Pygmy Shrew is Ireland's smallest mammal, weighing only 3 grammes in winter when food is scarce.

It has small eyes, which is probably why its Irish name 'Dallóg Fhraoigh' means 'blind animal of the heather'.

It is common all over Ireland where there is good ground cover. It likes grassland, hedgerows, woodland and bog.

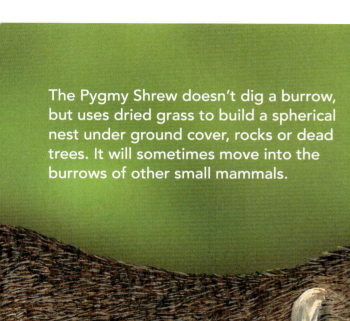

The Pygmy Shrew doesn't dig a burrow, but uses dried grass to build a spherical nest under ground cover, rocks or dead trees. It will sometimes move into the burrows of other small mammals.

The Pygmy Shrew is not a rodent like rats and mice, but an insectivore, related to other insect eaters like the Hedgehog.

SIZE

The Pygmy Shrew has a long pointed snout with long whiskers that twitch as it searches through leaf litter for food. It is a noisy animal, chattering as it moves about. It eats woodlice, beetles, flies, spiders, and insect larvae.

The Pygmy Shrew must keep busy to survive. Because it is so small it loses body heat more quickly than a larger animal so it must eat its own body weight in food every single day to stay alive. If it cannot find food for more than a few hours it will die. This means the Pygmy Shrew is active both night and day, all year round.

Rabbit

Coinín

The Rabbit is found all over Ireland on areas of short grass – on cliff tops, sand dunes, farmland, parks and gardens.

The Rabbit has large eyes on the sides of its head, giving it almost 360° vision – to help it to see predators coming from any direction. It has a white puffball tail called a 'scut' and long hind legs.

Rabbits live in family groups, and dig a large burrow system called a 'warren'. The warren is usually found at field edges, under hedgerows, brambles or scrub, where there is short grass nearby to graze. Rabbits also eat herbs such as dandelions and plantain.

A Rabbit Warren

Rabbits usually stay underground in their burrows during the day and come out after dark to feed, staying close to their warren so that they can quickly escape down a tunnel if threatened. When it senses danger, a Rabbit will thump its hind foot on the ground to warn other members of its family.

SIZE

The male Rabbit is called a 'buck', the female a 'doe' and young rabbits are called 'kittens'. Kittens are very helpless when they are born. They have no fur and their eyes are closed. They stay underground for the first three weeks of their lives.

Irish Mountain Hare

Giorria

The Irish Mountain Hare is unique to Ireland. It does not normally turn white in winter, unlike other hares in Europe. The Hare is much bigger than a Rabbit, with longer legs and ears. The hind feet are very long and it can run very fast.

The Hare is found on open farmland, uplands and grasslands. It is usually nocturnal but can be active during daylight hours in spring and summer. During the day, a hare usually rests above ground in a shallow dip in the ground called a 'form'.

Hopping Mad!

In spring, males and females are sometimes seen squabbling or fighting. They kick and box each other with their front legs and chase each other about. This led to the old saying 'as mad as a March Hare'.

SIZE

Male Hares are called 'jacks', females are called 'jills' and babies are called 'leverets'. Three or four leverets are born in a litter. The leverets are born with their eyes open and a full coat of fur. A few days after they are born they spread out and each leveret hides in a different form, only coming together once a day when their mother visits to feed them. This helps to stop a predator finding and killing all the leverets.

A baby 'leveret'

The Hare eats grasses, heather and herbs and will also browse on gorse, willow, bilberry and other shrubs.

Badger

Broc

The Badger is a beautiful animal with black stripes on its face. They are most active after dark. The male badger is called a 'boar', the female a 'sow', and the young are called 'cubs'.

Badgers eat plants and animals, so they are called 'omnivores'. Their main food is earthworms, which they dig from the earth, leaving shallow holes called 'snuffle holes'. They also eat beetles, snails, frogs, mushrooms, fruit, cereals and small mammals.

The Badger has five strong claws on each foot and is a great digger.

The Badger makes its home underground, digging long networks of tunnels and sleeping chambers called a 'sett'. Some setts are huge and have been used by badger families for hundreds of years.

They are very clean animals, regularly changing their bedding of dried grass and coming above ground to use latrines some distance from their sett as a toilet.

A Badger Sett

SIZE

Badgers live in family groups. Cubs are born below ground in spring and emerge from the sett for the first time at about seven weeks of age when they begin to explore the outside world.

During the winter months, Badgers become less active, spending more time underground, and on cool days their body temperature drops, in a process called 'torpor', so that they use less energy. But badgers don't hibernate which is a longer extended version of torpor.

The Otter has a very thick coat of fur next to its skin to keep it warm. This dense 'underfur' traps air to keep the skin dry.

The Otter is an excellent swimmer and has webbed toes to help it swim. Its long stiff whiskers help it find fish in murky water where it is difficult to see.

Otter

Madra Uisce

The Irish name for Otter is 'Madra Uisce' which means the 'water dog'.

Otters are found on rivers, lakes, wetlands, and around the coast. They mainly eat fish. Coastal otters also eat crabs, molluscs and sea urchins. The Otter holds its food between its paws while eating, sometimes, while lying on its back, using its belly as a table.

The Otter makes its home in the riverbank, digging a burrow called a 'holt'. A holt often has a number of entrances, some underwater.

The Otter usually lives alone, unless it is a mother with two or three cubs. It is territorial, meaning that one Otter controls one patch of the riverbank and its neighbour otter defends the next territory a few kilometres upstream. It marks its territory with its droppings, called 'spraints'.

Let's Play!

The Otter is a very playful animal. It uses the riverbank like a water slide, sliding down on its back or belly and then climbs up the bank to do it again!

Cubs wrestle with each other for fun and otters have been seen playing 'catch' with pebbles – it takes a pebble into its mouth and throws it up into the air just to catch it again.

Pine Marten

Cat crainn

The Irish name for the Pine Marten, Cat crainn, means 'tree cat' as this is a beautiful agile animal that spends much of its life in trees. Its long claws help it to climb and it can hold out its long fluffy tail for balance.

The Pine Marten is 'solitary', meaning it lives alone. It is usually active at night but females can sometimes be seen during daylight in the summer months as they hunt for extra food for their young. Up to five 'kits' are born in spring. Kits are blind and deaf at birth and rely completely on their mother for food.

This baby 'kit' was hand-reared at the Kildare Animal Foundation Wildlife Unit

SIZE

The Pine Marten eats fruit (such as blackberries), mushrooms, worms, insects, frogs, small mammals and birds, as well as dead animals it finds.

The Pine Marten often has a number of dens in its territory and may travel 20 kilometres in one night as it searches for food.

The Pine Marten uses a nest site or 'den' in hollow trees, crevices or rocks, large birds' nests, or squirrel dreys. It lines its nest with dried grass. It sometimes make its home in the roof of an old building.

The Irish Stoat looks different to stoats found in other countries and does not turn white in winter.

The Stoat is found in hedgerows, forest, moorland, marsh, scrub and upland areas. It has a long slim body and is very fast and agile. It is able to squeeze into very small burrows and rock crevices.

Irish Stoat

Easóg

The Stoat is quite a curious and playful animal. During spring and summer the Stoat is active during the day as well as after dark.

It is a master hunter. It can follow small mammals into their burrows and will follow over huge distances until it catches its target.

Look into my eyes!

The Stoat has a special trick it uses to help it catch a Rabbit, an animal 10 times its size. It 'hypnotises' it with a funny dance! It leaps about and stands on its hind legs and weaves its body in front of the Rabbit, which appears to go into a trance. Then the Stoat pounces, biting the back of the Rabbit's neck to kill it quickly. It carries away and hides food it doesn't eat straight away.

SIZE

Red Fox

Sionnach / Madra Rua

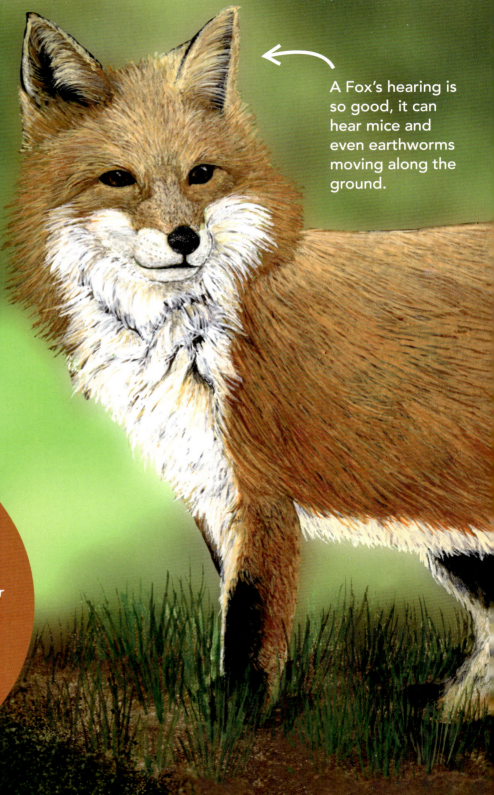

A Fox's hearing is so good, it can hear mice and even earthworms moving along the ground.

The Fox is a beautiful clever animal, and is a type of wild dog.

The male Fox is called a 'dog'; the female is called a 'vixen'; and the young are called 'cubs'. A Fox lives in a burrow known as a 'den' or 'earth'.

What does the Fox say?

A Fox doesn't bark like your pet dog. They are usually very quiet, but in winter the males and females communicate using sharp, high-pitched shrieks. These calls can sound like scary screams and may have led to tales of the 'banshee' in Ireland when, long ago, people heard a fox calling on a dark night.

A dog and vixen may stay together for a number of years. Their cubs are born each spring. For the first few weeks, the vixen stays with her cubs and the dog helps his family by bringing food back to the den.

Sometimes an 'aunt', a female from a previous litter will help rear the cubs, so the lucky cubs might have three adults looking after them in the family group.

As well as being a great runner and a very agile animal that can jump high walls and climb fences, the Fox can climb trees!

It has a varied diet. As well as mice, rats, rabbits, birds, eggs, and dead animals, they also eat insects, earthworms, and fruits such as blackberries and apples.

The Urban Fox

Some Foxes have learned to live in our towns and cities. They visit parks and gardens and have learned to find food humans throw away.

SIZE

Red Deer

Fia rua

The Red Deer is our largest land animal. The male, called a 'stag' is about 120cm tall at its shoulder. The female is called a 'hind' and the young are called 'calves'. The hind does not grow antlers and is smaller than the stag.

Red Deer are shy creatures that will quickly hide if disturbed. Stags and hinds usually live in separate groups except at rutting time, in autumn.

Red Deer eat lots of different foods, including grasses, herbs, acorns, woody shoots, and fruits.

The best place to see Red Deer in Ireland is Killarney National Park in Co. Kerry.

SIZE

The stag's large antlers are shed each spring and a new set starts to grow. They are fully grown by September. Each year the antlers grow larger, so you can recognise an older stag by the size of its antlers. Deer antlers are the fastest growing tissue of any mammal, and can grow an inch each day.

In September, the stags compete to become the boss! This is the rutting season. The stags wallow in the mud, making large puddles, called wallow holes, so that they smell very strongly. They also thrash their antlers against plants.

They roar deeply to display to other stags in a vocal contest. If a fight does break out, the stags clash their antlers together and push each other in either direction in a test of strength. The strongest stag becomes the father to all the calves born in that herd of hinds.

Sika Deer
Fia Seapánach

The male Sika Deer is called a 'stag', the female a 'hind', and young Sika are called 'calves'. Only the stags grow antlers, which are much smaller and have less points or 'tines' than those of the Red Deer.

Sika hinds live together in groups of up to 10 animals, usually made up of adult hinds, their daughters, and young calves. Stags live on their own but join the herd during the rut in autumn.

SIZE

During the summer, while the stag's antlers are growing, they are covered in a special skin called 'velvet' which falls off before the rut.

Deer eat grass and also browse on shrubs, leaves, fruit and brambles. Like cows and sheep, deer have special stomachs that allow them to eat plants that are difficult to digest. They bring their food back up to their mouths and chew it some more before swallowing it again. They usually rest and 'chew the cud', during the day, and come out of hiding to graze after dark.

Each spring, the buck sheds its antlers and a new set starts to grow. The antlers are fully grown by August.

Fallow Deer

Fia buí

SIZE

Fallow deer are our most widespread deer, and are found in every county in Ireland.

Male Fallow Deer are called 'bucks', females 'does' and young are called 'fawns'.

The Fallow Deer's coat varies from white to black, often with white spots along the back. Most have a white 'rump' patch on its bum. The Fallow Deer has a longer tail than the Red Deer or Sika Deer.

Fallow Deer form large herds. The bucks and does live in separate groups. The buck has beautiful 'palmate' antlers that grow flat and wide at the tips as the buck grows older.

Fallow Deer are found in deciduous woodland near grassy areas, where they can graze. They usually come out of cover early in the morning and just before dark to feed. As well as grass, they eat herbs, fruit and leaves.

Usually a doe gives birth to a single fawn in June. The fawn can stand up straight away when it is born – it is far more advanced than a human baby! This is so that it can run away from predators.

During its first two weeks of life, the fawn usually lies hidden in long grass, and its mother only makes short visits to give it milk. This helps to keep the fawn safe in its hiding place.

During the rut, the bucks clash antlers and wrestle to test their strength.

Common Pipistrelle Bat
Ialtóg fheascrach

There are over 1200 different types of bat, or bat 'species' in the world.

11 bat species have been recorded in Ireland. The Common Pipistrelle is the most frequently seen bat in this country. All Irish bats feed on insects and spiders.

SIZE

As blind as a bat?

Contrary to myths about bats, bats are not blind. They have good eyesight, like humans, but to help them fly and find their food in the pitch dark, they use a special sense humans don't have, called 'echolocation'.

To echolocate, the bat emits high-pitched calls that humans cannot hear and these sounds bounce off objects back to the bat's sensitive ears so that the bat can build a picture of its surroundings. This allows a bat to chase down flying insects and fly at 15 kilometres per hour in complete darkness!

Bats may travel three kilometres from their daytime roost in a single night as they search for food. The Common Pipistrelle is one of our smallest bats, its head and body measuring only 4 centimetres in length, and weighing only about 6 grammes! But they are strong flyers!

During the day, bats sleep, hanging upside down in a cool, safe place, called a bat roost. Just before sunset, they fly out of their roost to hunt for insects. Bats hunt in woodland, over farmland, rivers and lakes.

 The Pipistrelle Bat catches flies, midges, and moths. A Pipistrelle Bat can catch over 3,000 midges in one night!

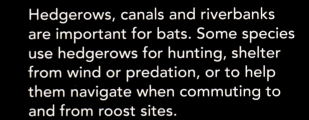

Hedgerows, canals and riverbanks are important for bats. Some species use hedgerows for hunting, shelter from wind or predation, or to help them navigate when commuting to and from roost sites.

Bats fly with their fingers!

A bat's wing has evolved from the skin and elongated forearm and hand bones. One Irish name for the bat 'sciathán leathair' means 'leather wing'.

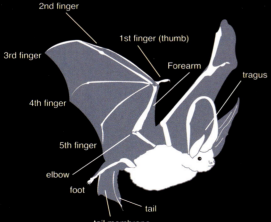

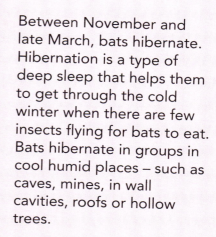

SIZE

Between November and late March, bats hibernate. Hibernation is a type of deep sleep that helps them to get through the cold winter when there are few insects flying for bats to eat. Bats hibernate in groups in cool humid places – such as caves, mines, in wall cavities, roofs or hollow trees.

Brown Long-Eared Bat

Ialtóg fhad-chluasach

It's not hard to see where this bat got its name! Its ears are almost as long as its body! The Brown Long-Eared Bat whispers its echolocation calls.

Sometimes it doesn't need to use echolocation at all in order to find its prey – instead, its large powerful ears actually allow it to 'hear' insects. They can follow the sound and catch an insect in the pitch dark.

Lesser Horseshoe Bat

Ialtóg crúshrónach / Crú-ialtóg beag

The Lesser Horseshoe Bat has a horseshoe-shaped 'nose leaf' around its nostrils. They echolocate through their nostrils and the disc-like shape of the noseleaf is thought to help them direct their echolocation calls.

Lesser Horseshoe Bats are excellent at flying! They can whizz in and out of branches using their very flexible wings.

Lesser Horseshoe Bats hunt in woodlands, feeding mainly on flies and midges. They feed by aerial 'hawking' – catching insects on the wing – and 'gleaning' – picking insects from vegetation.

SIZE

The Lesser Horseshoe Bat hangs freely from its feet, often with its wings wrapped around its body.

A mother and baby bat.

Each spring, female bats gather in a 'maternity roost' to have their young. There can be over 100 female bats in a maternity colony. Between June and July, the female gives birth to one baby bat.

The baby is born without fur so the maternity roost where they are born must be dry and warm.

The mother bat hangs upside down, while the baby clings to her 'right side up'! If the colony is in danger, the mother may carry her baby to a new roost. Like all mammals the baby bat is fed with mother's milk. By mid-August the baby starts to fly and catch insects for itself. A bat may live for up to 30 years!

Grey Seal

Rón mór

There are two types of seal in Irish waters, the Grey Seal and the Harbour/Common Seal. The Grey Seal is the most frequently seen seal around Irish coasts.

The Grey Seal is a big heavy animal, the male can grow to 3 metres in length and can weigh 300kg. That's about four times the weight of a man.

The male is called a 'bull', the female a 'cow' and the babies are called 'pups'. Seals eat fish, squid and crustaceans.

A grey seal pup has bright white fur when it is born and it can't swim until it gets its new darker waterproof coat when it is about three weeks old.

In September each year Grey Seals gather in large colonies to have their pups. The cows return to the same beach every year and even the same spot on the shore to have their pup. The colony is a noisy place where the seals moan, rumble and bark to each other.

SIZE

Seals have a special layer of blubber under the skin to help keep them warm in cold water.

Its eyes are specially adapted to help it see underwater. In murky water, or down deep, where less light reaches from the surface, the seal's long sensitive whiskers help it to sense the movements of fish.

Mother and pup have a very strong bond from birth. The cow recognises her pup by its scent and its call. The mother stays close to her pup for the first few weeks of its life. She doesn't go to sea to hunt so she loses a lot of weight.

A Grey Seal can dive to depths of 70 metres underwater when searching for food, and can stay underwater for 16 minutes at a time.

Harbour Seal
Rón breacach (beag)

The Harbour Seal is also sometimes called the Common Seal. It varies in colour from beige to dark grey with dark patches. The Harbour Seal has big round eyes and long whiskers to help it hunt for fish underwater.

The seal's feet have become webbed flippers. It might look like a very awkward animal on land but underwater the seal's streamlined body and flippers make it a brilliant swimmer.

Seals can often be seen lying up on rocks or sandbanks around the Irish coast. Seals come onto land to have their pups, to bask in the sun or when they are 'moulting' – getting a new fur coat – but they actually spend most of their time in the sea. They can even sleep in the water, positioning themselves upright, and bobbing up and down in the waves, which we call 'bottling'.

Grey Seal or Harbour Seal?

The Grey Seal is larger than the Harbour Seal. It also has a flatter head and longer nose, with nostrils that are almost parallel to each other, while the Harbour Seal's nostrils form a V-shape.

Pups are usually born in July, much earlier than grey seal pups. Harbour Seals don't form large breeding colonies like Grey Seals.

The Harbour Seal pup looks like a miniature version of its mother. It already has its waterproof fur and blubber to keep it warm, so it can start to swim straight after birth.

SIZE

Harbour Porpoise

Muc mhara

This is not a fish, it is a marine mammal called a Cetacean. The whales and dolphins are Cetaceans. 24 types or species of whales and dolphins have been seen in Irish waters.

Like all mammals, Cetaceans must breathe air and the mother feeds its young, called a 'calf', with its milk.

The Harbour Porpoise is the most frequently seen Cetacean found around Ireland and it's also our smallest, growing to just 1.7 metres long.

Like bats, some Cetaceans use their sense of hearing to help find their food. The animal makes clicking sounds that bounce off objects such as fish and return to the dolphin or whale. Its brain can draw a 'sound picture' of their surroundings using their hearing. This is called 'echolocation'.

SIZE

Like all whales and dolphins, the Porpoise has a thick layer of blubber under the skin to help it keep warm.

The Irish name for the Harbour Porpoise is 'Muc mhara' or 'Sea pig' because of its short round body.

Porpoises live in groups of up to 10 animals. Calves are born in the summer months. When a baby dolphin or whale is born, its mother pushes it up to the surface so that it can take its first breath of air. It breathes through its blowhole – the nostril on top of its head.

45

Common Dolphin

Deilf / Dorad

The Common Dolphin is a very playful animal. If you are travelling by boat off the Irish Coast, Common Dolphins will often show up and 'bow ride', riding the crest of the waves created by the bow at the front of the boat as it moves through the water.

They also jump into the air, clear of the water, which we call 'breaching'. They can turn somersaults in the air, which looks like they are having great fun.

SIZE

Common Dolphins live in a large group called a 'pod'. Sometimes these pods can become huge, and 2,000 Common Dolphins have been seen swimming together.

The Common Dolphin is one of our most colourful dolphins, with a large yellow patch on each side of its body.

It makes lots of sounds, including clicks and buzzes for echolocation and high-pitched whistles for communicating with other dolphins.

Bottlenose Dolphin

Deilf Bolgshrónach

Bottlenose Dolphins are very playful, sociable animals that live in groups of about 15 animals and will help each other if they are in danger.

There are lots of bottlenose dolphins living around our coasts. About 100 bottlenose dolphins have been recorded living in the Shannon Estuary.

The Bottlenose Dolphin can dive down to 300 metres below the surface. They usually hunt fish that live near the sea floor so they are found near land where the water is more shallow than the open ocean. They often hunt in groups, helping each other to herd small fish into tight groups called 'bait-balls' so they are easier to catch.

Dolphins breaching

SIZE

A dolphin has lots of sharp teeth which help it to catch slippery fish. Once it grabs a fish in its beak it flips it to the back of its mouth and swallows the fish whole, as it can't chew.

A mother and baby dolphin have a very close bond. The calf stays close to its mother for up to six years. It becomes an adult at 10 years old and may live to 50.

Orca/Killer Whale

Cráin Dubh

The Killer Whale or Orca is a toothed whale like the Bottlenose Dolphin and is the largest member of the dolphin family, weighing up to 10 tonnes.

It is known as the Killer Whale because it hunts other whales, dolphins and seals as well as fish.

Orcas live in groups of up to 40 animals. The group is called a 'pod'. They are very intelligent animals and hunt together as a group which helps them to catch large prey.

SIZE

An adult male can reach over 9 metres in length and its large dorsal fin can be 2 metres tall – taller than a man!

The Orca is one of the fastest swimmers on Earth. It can reach speeds of over 50 kilometres per hour. Its smooth skin and streamlined shape helps it to move quickly through the water.

The Orca can follow prey for hundreds of kilometres. As the animal they are chasing gets tired, it becomes easier to catch.

Humpback Whale

Míol Mór Dronnach

The Humpback Whale is found in oceans all over the world and is a regular visitor to Irish waters.

The Humpback Whale can reach 16 metres in length. As it dives underwater, the whale arches its back and this is how it got the name 'humpback'.

Humpback Whales migrate huge distances across the globe, travelling thousands of miles to give birth to their young in warmer waters.

Humpbacks sometimes use a very clever hunting technique known as 'bubble-netting'. One or two Humpbacks will swim up under a shoal of fish, while spiralling and blowing out bubbles. This causes the fish to swim into the centre of this bubble ring. Then the huge whale swims up through the bubble net with its huge mouth wide open and engulfs the fish!

SIZE

The Humpback Whale is well known for its 'song', producing the longest, most complex sounds of all the whales and dolphins. Some sounds are like long moans, others are whistles, clicks and chirps.

It is the male whale that sings and it may use these songs to attract females and warn off other males during the breeding season.

It is believed that other whales may be able to hear the Humpback's song from 150 kilometres away.

Its flippers, on the sides of its body, are very long and can reach 5 metres in length. Its head is also very big, making up one-third of its total body length.

Fin Whale

Míol mór eiteach

The Fin Whale has been called the 'greyhound of the sea' because its long sleek body cuts through the water at great speed as it cruises along at about 40 kilometres per hour.

It is the world's second largest animal, growing to 27 metres long. Fin whales are seen each year off the Waterford and Cork coasts.

The Fin Whale does not have teeth. Instead, it has long strips of tough springy combs in its jaws called 'baleen plates' which it uses to sieve krill and small fish from the water. Whales with baleen instead of teeth, such as the Humpback Whale, Minke Whale, and Blue Whale, are called 'baleen whales'.

Baleen plates

SIZE

Like all baleen whales, the Fin Whale has a pair of blowholes. These can be fully closed during dives underwater so they are completely airtight.

When hunting the Fin Whale can dive to 470 metres below the surface and can stay underwater for up to 15 minutes. It sometimes circles fish at high speed to form what is called a 'bait ball' before swimming into it, mouth open.

It can open its jaws very wide and engulf a huge amount of water and fish. It then closes its jaws and pushes the water back out of the mouth through its baleen, which allows the water to leave but traps the fish.

Baleen whales can live to 80 or 90 years of age.

Blue Whale

Míol mór gorm

The Blue Whale is the largest animal on earth. The Irish name means 'big blue beast'.

It is difficult to get your head around how big this animal is. It weighs up to 170 tonnes, the same as 30 African elephants! And it can grow up to 33 metres in length!

The baby Blue Whale is 8 metres in length when it is born – about the same length as a bus! During the first 7 months of its life, the calf will drink 400 litres of milk a day from its mother.

The grunting sound of a Blue Whale is louder than the sound of a space rocket taking off!

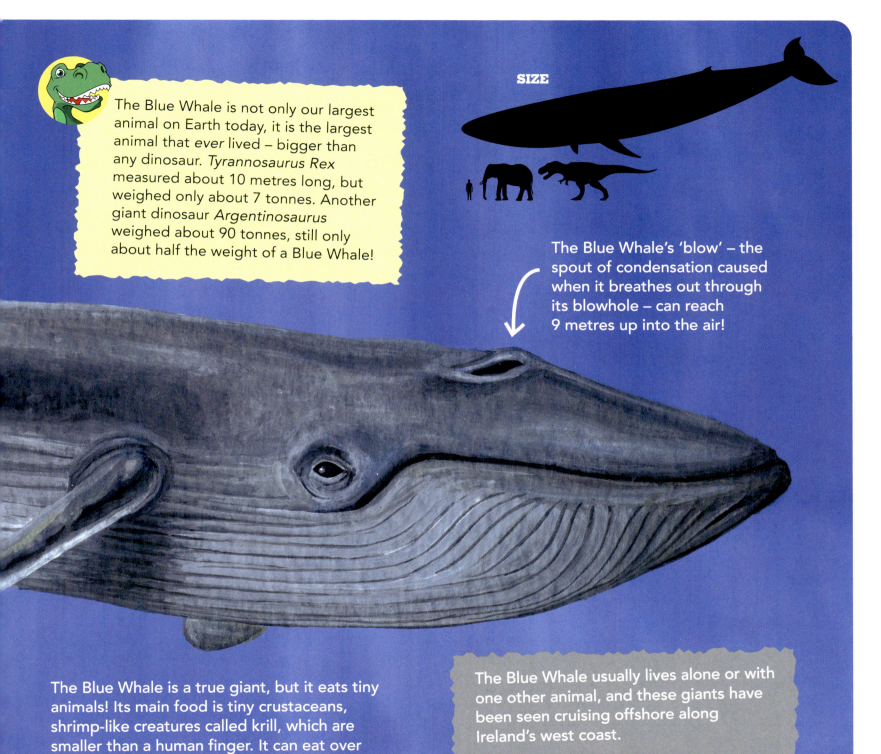

The Blue Whale is not only our largest animal on Earth today, it is the largest animal that *ever* lived – bigger than any dinosaur. *Tyrannosaurus Rex* measured about 10 metres long, but weighed only about 7 tonnes. Another giant dinosaur *Argentinosaurus* weighed about 90 tonnes, still only about half the weight of a Blue Whale!

SIZE

The Blue Whale's 'blow' – the spout of condensation caused when it breathes out through its blowhole – can reach 9 metres up into the air!

The Blue Whale is a true giant, but it eats tiny animals! Its main food is tiny crustaceans, shrimp-like creatures called krill, which are smaller than a human finger. It can eat over 3,000kg of krill or 40 million of these tiny animals in one day.

The Blue Whale usually lives alone or with one other animal, and these giants have been seen cruising offshore along Ireland's west coast.

A note for parents/teachers

TIPS TO HELP WILDLIFE

(and help your children connect with nature)

Wildlife faces many threats, including pollution, climate change, invasive species, and habitat loss and fragmentation through changing farming practices and the construction of roads and buildings. But there are lots of things you can do to help your local wildlife.

Here are some ideas.

Don't keep your garden too 'tidy'. Let corners of your garden or schoolyard grow wild, and you will see native grasses, herbs and wild flowers spring up. This will provide homes for lots of small creatures which in turn provide food for our birds and mammals. A patch of young nettles becomes a home and food supply for Peacock, Red Admiral and Tortoiseshell butterfly caterpillars; while a pile of leaves or logs left in a sheltered corner of your garden may provide a nest place for a hibernating hedgehog over winter.

Don't mow your roadside verges. If you live in the countryside, that strip of land at the side of the road could be a refuge for many of our insects and small creatures that are pushed out of farmland and manicured gardens. Many of our bumblebees are disappearing and unmanaged roadside verges can provide important sources of nectar for these wonderful insects that go on to help humans by pollinating our food crops.

Feed the birds. Putting up bird feeders in your garden or school yard over winter is a lovely way to observe birds at close quarters and fitting bird boxes will make them even more welcome.

Create new habitats. Plant a wildlife garden. Make a bug hotel in your school. A garden pond will attract frogs and newts. Plant buddleia or the 'butterfly bush', lilac, and honeysuckle to provide nectar for butterflies. Plant lavender or marjoram to attract bees.

Putting up a bat box creates a safe place for bats to roost, and you will get to watch the bats coming and going each evening. They will also keep your local midges at bay. Bat boxes can be placed on a tree or wall, around your school. By the way, if you discover you have bats living in your attic, you don't need to worry. Bats do not damage property. They don't gnaw wood or bring in nesting material. They simply hang head down from the roof. Bat droppings consist of powdered insect fragments and are not a danger to health.

Plant native trees and hedgerows. By planting Irish trees and plants in your garden you will naturally encourage your local wildlife, offering new sources of food and shelter. This is also a great way to bring nature into your school. By keeping your native hedge or planting native species in a new hedge, you are helping many animals that use hedgerows. It is very important not to cut your hedge during the bird nesting season. It is illegal to cut between March 1st and August 31st each year.

Avoid garden chemicals. Insecticides and slug pellets can kill far more animals than the ones that might be eating your plants. Many small mammals, birds and amphibians rely on insects for food. Poisons accumulated can harm animals that eat insects such as bats and hedgehogs. Pesticides can also pollute our watercourses.

Get to know your local wildlife. Your nearest parks, woodlands, nature reserves, nature education centres and national parks are a great place to start. Of course, wildlife isn't confined to just our large parks. Those small wildlife patches in your area – such as a country laneway, an old graveyard, a local stream, or a wasteland that has been taken over by wild flowers – may be very important for wildlife. Encourage local park managers to leave patches for wildlife.

Start wildlife-watching with your children. Get some binoculars, rain gear and wellies, and get outdoors and explore. We often complain about how much time children spend in front of screens, so why not bring your child outdoors to meet nature and help them make that connection. It might just be good for you too – in fact, it's been proven, a connection with nature is good for your health!

Go beachcombing; explore a rockpool; encourage them to climb a tree; build a den; have a conker fight; help them find animal tracks and droppings. Get your children to start a wildlife journal to record their adventures. When you're wildlife watching, enjoy the small things. Even if you don't get to see that elusive Pine Marten on your first try, seeing garden birds, a rabbit or even bugs and spiders can be great fun! Every day spent with nature can offer something new.

Join a wildlife club or conservation group. A great way to learn more about nature while also helping your local wildlife is to join a wildlife conservation charity. Becoming a member means you can attend their nature events and receive their magazines, and at the same time you're supporting their conservation projects. Or ask your school about attending a nature event or arrange a school visit from a wildlife expert through the Heritage in Schools Programme.

There is so much out there to try – help with a river or beach clean-up or go on a nature walk with the Irish Wildlife Trust; go to a Dawn Chorus event; learn to identify insects with the National Biodiversity Data Centre; take part in a bird survey with Birdwatch Ireland; join an Ulster Wildlife Trust Wildlife Club; or why not go whale-watching with the Irish Whale and Dolphin Group. A love of nature is a wonderful gift to pass on to your children. So get outdoors and enjoy!

Useful Websites:

Green Schools
www.greenschoolsireland.org

An Taisce – The National Trust
www.antaisce.org

BirdWatch Ireland
www.birdwatchireland.ie

Bat Conservation Ireland
www.batconservationireland.org

The Heritage Council
www.heritagecouncil.ie

Heritage in Schools Programme
www.heritageinschools.ie

Herpetological Society of Ireland (Reptiles and Amphibians)
www.thehsi.org

Irish Peatland Conservation Council
www.ipcc.ie

Irish Whale and Dolphin Group
www.iwdg.ie

Irish Wildlife Trust
www.iwt.ie

National Parks & Wildlife Service
www.npws.ie

National Biodiversity Data Centre
www.biodiversityireland.ie

Natural History Museum
www.museum.ie/naturalhistory

Royal Society for the Protection of Birds
www.rspb.org.uk

Ulster Wildlife Trust
www.ulsterwildlifetrust.org

The Vincent Wildlife Trust
www.vwt.org.uk

About the author

JUANITA BROWNE

I always loved animals so when I went to college I studied Zoology – wild animals and their biology. I love sharing stories about wildlife and the natural world, so I have worked on wildlife magazines and books, including 'Ireland's Mammals', published in 2005. I now work on Natural History documentaries for television and radio. Sometimes I visit primary schools to talk about wildlife. This is my fourth book. I really hope you enjoy it.

About the illustrator

AOIFE QUINN

I am a twenty four year old artist from Wicklow. I studied in the National College of Art and Design and graduated with a BA in craft design in 2012. The main focus of my art has always centred on nature. Through my paintings and illustrations I aim to celebrate this, as well as create an awareness of the vulnerability of many of the animals and insects I depict.